controlled burn

controlled burn

A. Frances Johnson

Puncher & Wattmann

First published in 2025
Published by Puncher & Wattmann
PO Box 279
Waratah NSW 2298

info@puncherandwattmann.com

A catologue record for this book is available from The National Library of Australia.

ISBN 9781923099708

Cover design by David Musgrave

Cover image: Peter Gardiner, *Black Lung* (*Black Lung* series, 2017)

Printed by Lightning Source International

Contents

Part 1: controlled burn

Part 2: headfire

how many books
did I burn? | scores |

whose books? | whose books
did you burn? |

reader, I burnt yours

– Simon Armitage, 'Before the raised eyebrows'

Part 1:
controlled burn

Optimism™

On this one perfect day
I know that ALDI will run a special
on defibrillators in aisle three,
specials on extinct species
and banned books in aisle four,
that I can lie down in aisle six
with its fridges of frozen greens
as if in a forest and feel safe
and indestructible as trolleys
crammed with cheap brie.
I know aircon will screen out
smoke haze suffocating
the thick-windowed city,
that I'll be double-glaze happy
over quenchable shelves of cheap soda
that can put anything out, anything at all,
that delivery trucks will make it
down the blistered highways
to assuage my every need,
that I am waiting for them as usual,
ready to pounce on the special day,
and that on such a good, plentiful day,
the order to evacuate will not come.

Mice and men

Our father wore Glo-Weave permanent press.
Pinned in boxes with pearl-tipped pins, manly shirts
distributed nationwide, creases ironed out
to suggest 24-hour invincibility, sharp futures.
Don't get ideas, laughed my mother, settling
into a lungful of sherry on slave's night off.
We set our sights not on the shirts but on the boxes.
Inside them, my brother and I built and glued
cardboard mazes, arranging cunning cheddar lures.
The walls were erratically scaled and cut by chubby fingers;
what did we know about life's general obstructions?
Our wily navigators would secure the prize.
We scheduled the race for Saturday morning, after the cartoons
and before the sword-and-sandal epic
with its gleaming charioteers.

In our dark garage stood a blanketed bird cage
full of sheared newspapers and sawdust, plastic bowls
and tiny circus wheel. Our mice never used the wheel
like showy TV mice in white-coat experiments.
The cage looked empty, a sawdust and paper thoroughfare
as desolate as the kind a killer in a Western rides through.
I topped up water and food. Don't do that, my father growled,
they're breeding like crazy, we can't keep them.
A burgeoning city of mice slumbered underneath
the layered shavings, disguising procreative gift.
To peer inside, seven days after a litter birthed,
was to discover a dim Catholic universe of blind and deaf pinkies,
huddled like fomenting marshmallows in a sweet, sickly stink.
We stroked the pups' rosy noses and ears, curving
our starfish hands into tiny cribs. Could red eyes
really be that gentle? And the hard question I had not asked

our father, faint sweat stain creeping round
his permanent-press collar: who would keep them?

The day came when my brother was roped in, a manly rite,
to help drown them. My mother cried in the kitchen
because my brother was crying, the role of small-killer-
come-to-town did not fit her darling red-nosed boy.
He wore no funeral black, just faded green tracksuit bottom,
was neither murderer nor suburban Lenny.
Our father gave us a talk, stentorian and uneasy,
drumming thick fingers against a mug of warm Milo.
It's like this, he said. Mice are breeding machines.
They gestate between nineteen to twenty-one days.
We're looking at ten births a year, ten to fourteen pups a time.
We can't keep them. The word 'zoo' lurched into my head,
shorter than 'sanctuary', but my psychic mother shook her head,
refilled her sorrowful glass and dragged me into a hug.
The task required two buckets, running water, a shovel,
a deep hole at the end of the garden, one ten-year-old boy
and one fifty-year-old man given to bitter musings
about passage through the maze of life. Nothing in life
was pearl-tipped, cheesily victorious, his set mouth said.
Inside the cold dark garage, the men picked up blind pup
after pup by the tails and dropped them into freezing pails
like rose-tipped snowballs. My mother and I sat stock still
at the kitchen table. I felt my throat button down
as if a cardboard gate lodged there, that feel
of permanent press, the first run of loss,
my heart spinning on, a small unridden wheel.

Controlled burn

The silent man, her neighbour,
who is always paid more for less,
stock and field, has a mouth full
of clattering silver, jowls that shudder
pilgrim entitlement, gouty wrath.
He breathes in the smoke-blanketed valley,
choreographs rollies in quiet,
practised strikes. With men,
he's loquacious, a trough tap
turned on. He calls them all up –
her practise burn must be argued against,
her stream access and water rights.
Fire is bitch, as he sees it. Practising
controlled burns a fool's idea. By Christ,
he repeats, but he can't make it rhyme.
His new neighbour is a bad spot fire,
something to be put out, hosed down,
like the boys mucking about river pastures
in his grandad's rifling time.

But he underestimates her cool
melancholy, the science and law
undergirding her decision not to sell,
to stay and defend when fire
rushes uphill to burn
down the poet's desk
and make shed iron sing.
She won't be put out.
Let him cut down every tree,
suck the fire brigade dry –
there's no room in her bunker for him.

Setting the table

I set the table as bearded heath
and prickly moses lean in,
forming radiant mosh pits
in late spring understoreys.
Veranda boards buckle in the heat,
we'll eat inside I think. Salads.
I don't bother with butter knives,
bone handled, the whole country
a drawer full of unmarked bones.
I dream of resting my cheek
against the day-moon's
pale-faced expiation.
But I have work to do.
Knives, forks and serviettes are laid out
in funerary style. Proud lemon cake.
You are down in the north paddock,
moving fretting stock to lower ground
by the dam. It's taking too long.
I set dessert spoons, then remove them.

When the first low branches ignite,
I think of city pyrotechnics, festival claps,
not rare orchids conceding, nodding doom.
In town, children in animal-print pyjamas
are marched down a lone asphalt street
through rec centre doors, solemn
as fun-palace teeth.
Inside, the sports court
Is dulled to churchy gloom.
We had booked a place there.

I wait and wait; there is only one
road in and out. Suddenly, witches

roar bitter carbon songs
in the trees. There's no sunset clause,
no chemist-shop balm for colonial heat.
I leave no note – paper is fuel, not love.
I climb into the bath with wet wool
blankets, slab of yellow cake and phone.
The whiff of eucalypt and water calms.
Look! My mother, hanging out sheets
and clouds against a sky too cruel, too blue
to look at. And I am a child's jumper
on washing day, arms flailing free,
waiting to be unpegged.

The woman who ran the farm

Introduce a slope of small
degree and wildfire burns,
a quick path to the wooden desk.
Introduce a clever woman.
See her forecast inquisitions
of fire and words. She's raced
past two dead husbands –
each liking a bet and a pint,
a purpling Rorschach punch.
She knows the burnt parts
of history, spot fires of disbelief
connect her canopy of days
to the fencepost's grey despair.
She races past her hot tin sheds;
their pinging siren songs won't save.
She can't outrun the livid forest,
a season of fuse and tripwire.

Still, she limits her sprint
as if to segment fate, trade chances,
freeing butting stock as she passes
the boiling lake. Wire cutting
slows her down; sideways eyes
rim with panic and woolly trust
as shins smoulder in insectless yellow grass.
Mask askew, she recalls documents,
chaste and white, on the dash
of the exploding ute. Hear her
howl at this rare stupidity.
Call it temperament, call her victim,
crazy-for-not-leaving. Call her witch.
She won't leave her animals, won't sell
cheap to the jawless neighbour.

Now the cattle are in the lake,
alive and safe. Soon she'll be with them.
But the candled understorey
closes in, a birthday surprise.
The lake disappears in red-roiled smoke.
In the north paddock, furies rise,
throats buttoned down by fire.
Her mother and grandmother
have each played their bitter part
and handed it to her, as if this was always
the place to start, run from and finish in.
Wear an ironed blouse, they wail,
you never know who you'll meet.
But this is the devil's dancefloor,
she thinks, dam bubbling vestigial hope,
the calves' stricken choir renouncing teats,
grassy memory. She sprints through
smoke, a singed Diana, if only to be
her last, best potential, fuelled by
a dream of sleep, animals softly lowing,
calling her to green pastures.

Inheritance

Gadabanud Country, Lighthouse Road

I will not leave my animals as you left me.
I remember your shadow tractor flying
over rutted cloud towards a bookie sun,
too keen to bet on hardened pastures,
boiled dams and end-time fire events.
Well, not quite 'over'; you passed through
cloud and evening's remnant aurora
in your sweat-browned busted straw hat,
over paddocks furrowed like brows,
your dicky ventricles flunking
their last sheepdog trial, that wild race
of blood, hope and efficiency
pegging us to time and pilfered place,
our bleating creatures in sensurround,
gnawing cocksfoot, ryegrass, phalaris –
empire's weedy carpets.

I backhoe Patterson's curse for days
after your funeral, burning off
its mauve-emerald grip on a Sunday pyre.
I clean slimy gutters and water tanks
as if my life depends on it, won't pay
young men from town to help
nor listen to our sockless city son,
he of the neat suits and pale side part
who roars up one weekend to wrestle
the filing cabinet's blank refusals
of poetry: 'going into administration';
'greenfield development'; 'bankruptcy'.
I know that he'll soon force the matter,
neaten time into a rhymeless deal.

He stares at my white hair and papery skin,
my mothering surface, a paper to sign.
Then we raise a glass to you, love,
but one of us gets the ryegrass staggers.

I say, as he leaves, that I'm still strong enough
to tackle all the invasive creep in the valley –
the gin-cup neighbour who won't burn
gorse or curse, faded print of Streeton's
Early Summer: Gorse in Bloom
on his mantel, grandfather's guns
hung north, south, east and west
like objets d'art, not evidence.
I've already signed away half the land,
sharing the precious bore with a hobby farmer
who forgets to turn off the tap.
My son folds me into a city-suit hug
and I ask myself, to whom do I now declare
the tractored bone and midden,
the history of a road pushed through
forest like a slow shot,
the unquiet archive, hidden?

Lamb, calf, crow

Pretty lambs, bottle fed,
gambol over abattoir contracts.
The bravest is born nodding
his boofy head over and over,
as if to agree that hooved rapture
is an unstoppable algorithm
others will surely pay for.
When the soil sets diamond hard,
colonial recipe books come out –
see moderate bake
after immoderate death.
We are all braised blue;
the thing is to use all parts of the body.

Now hot wind soughs through
blank, dense understoreys.
Under conditions of loss,
all creatures herd, wondering
what error their mother made
to be disappeared.
On singing wires, crows
chant the same blank syllable
as animals cram
into layer-cake trucks
where fear equates
proportionally
with lack of space,
the iron taste
of productivity's shadow.

Snake versus human

The path rears up, not the snake, a false picturesque.
Your role is to play foreground fencepost
until perspective slithers back, prelapsarian throwback.
In this moment, split from all other moments,
a coiling flutter in your overscaled hips
recalls lost swamp time, desire to glide.
Midground at noon is all sandy rut, flanked
by meshed sedge and bracken, crazed shadow.
A disaster of heat pins you like warm felt.
Your dog enslaved on a tight lead is not felt.
He yelps why? Why? Why can't he bolt forward
and lift his leg on this thin-poured red-bellied black,
reward himself with a nugget of marsupial scat?
Because you, colonial Eve, suppress knowledge
of the orchard that grew the wise snake,
drawing dark brushmarks through sand
on a bright, path-rearing Monday. Breathe the line
and watch it glide through remnant bracken,
little birds and mice tearing frantically away
from its cursive envenomation.
You rush through its shadow-paved world
and know that you are still half asp and Eden,
half flight and fight,
destroyer of creaturely refugia.
You refuse your dog leashless freedom
as you refuse self-knowledge, grinding down
your own milk fangs, unsure what
tempted you now as then, hips
coiling and sinking in a fallen world.

Aqua nullius

Mourning breaks
on the drained Murray–Darling,
rivermouth flossed by tides.
Nearby, unshy mallee fowls
forget song and mound,
show off pretty rust wings.
Tourists phone in sightings.

In gaitered language, poets
drag pens through Coorong sand,
form failed impressions
of helixed goanna trails.
In city offices, 'Water Security'
patterns the stapled page,
floods the line undivined,
except by riverine nations
fighting for water.
In blistered sheds, cheap-fix schemes
flip like burgers.
When the Murri hydrogeologist
arrives, landowners in Land Rovers,
rain-striped suits and mirror shades,
perform stakeholder dances
as mottled scrub chicks chant:
what's-at-stake, at-stake at-stake.

Aquifers, unschooled in buybacks,
lean in, teach flow and absence
of flow, cycle and consequence.
When officials propose a museum
of lost water, Barkindji songs
whistle through dust-cut beds,
groundwater dry-drowns.

Oh wide Murrundi, Barka,
Millewa and Indi. Shrug off
the polyester name 'Murray',
the raping moniker 'Darling'.
Close off the mythic faucet
of aqua nullius, and return
and return, flowing home.

Note: For First Nations scholar Virginia Marshall, government failures to enshrine Indigenous water rights and interests in legislation directly reflects Australia's western framing of Indigenous land rights, as shaped by the doctrine of 'terra nullius', whereby Indigenous water rights are reconstructed as 'aqua nullius' or 'water belonging to no one' (2016). Marshall V. (2016), 'Deconstructing aqua nullius: Reclaiming Aboriginal water rights and communal identity in Australia', *Indigenous Law Bulletin*, vol. 8 (26), 9–13.

Eel race

Dights Falls, Wurundjeri Country

1.
At the dock, hold-blind rabbits explode
from gunpowder stores, moving upriver,
to eat out understorey cures and salves.
Hatless ghosts crash through eucalypt,
kangaroo grass hooking calico and felt
in cordite-fugged air.

2.
The hatless, crimes unaccounted for,
build weirs over beer-toned river,
guts loose with bread and hops.
Reedy Yarra notes find their glottal stop,
while in town, big dough rises white and soft,
but never enough to appease or fill.

3.
River creatures become rare silver.
Old stories divert at the new mill,
crazed with jade weed and ivy. On Sundays,
bell-skirted ghosts set up en plein air,
dash off unreliable watercolours
of stone, flour and leaf
for parlours that tick, tick, tick.

4.
Wurundjeri, pushed upriver, divert anger
into diplomacy. But possum-cloaked grandeur
can't arrest the fancy kill of survey ink.
Captain Hoddle rests his quill,
sends orders to strongarm the bent river.

His shot glass holds a bullet, a dram of fantasy.
Weary history, crouched bankside, pegs out
salt-stiff underclothes under musket sun
and waits for him to come.

5.
A century on, a steel fishway is touted
(the sump can't be disturbed). By 4pm,
clipboards and lanyards wilt; freeway fumes
form a vast dirty crinoline
beneath the sun's CEO leer.
The meeting adjourns for a decade.

6.
2011. Eels dream a flow future,
but acknowledgement of country
is white noise. Expectations low,
they founder merrily, merrily
against the old weir, gasp on silt
above the water line. No upstream
story helps them make the pass.

The sentence

after 'Verdicts' by Dmitri Prigov

Eucalyptus regnans, aka Mountain Ash,
is sentenced to be culled for obstructing
logging machinery and quad bikes
in cool temperate zones and snowline tiers.
The cleared view is within our sights; we won't
countenance co-option of the word 'green',
wood-headed blockades led by children.

Rose Mallee, notorious honey pot
(true name E. rodantha), is sentenced
to ten years for open straggling,
for allowing numbers to fall into 50% decline,
for failing to protect thinned understorey
on degraded verges and consorting
openly with introduced serrated tussock.

E. molucanna, aka the thuggish Grey Box,
shall be sentenced to oblivion for gathering
in remnant groups of seven or more,
insisting upon the Dharawul species name
'terriyergro', and for inculcating voters
with eerie memories of riverine landscape.

E. morrisby (or Morrisby's gum) is, with
twenty-nine extant family members,
charged with negligence on two counts:
submission to drought and to dieback, ex-situ
sub-populations inclusive. Hereby sentenced
to functional extinction. Do not doubt, stands
will be taken against natural stands.

The pale Manna (E. Viminalis), for conscientious
objection, is sentenced to be shot at dawn,
unsightly ghost trunks sawn and removed.
Remnant juve trees shall receive custodial time
for enabling leaf-stripping by re-introduced koalas,
thereby failing to uphold the Latin epithet
'pliant twig' and the weeping habit of branches.

Harsh sentences will be handed down for
members who collude with the above genus:
colluding substrates, rivers and aquifers etc.
For such bitter crimes against the state
and its allies, country will be fracked
until it cries for mercy, catchments mined
until the dry earth, too, is arraigned
dockside and forced to explain.

Shallow-rooted stress in the dock
will be noted, but do not ask for water
or remand in uncompacted soil
(though clerk of courts hasten with
empty glass for candid photo opp).
We shall apply the beneficent rule of law
and leave no stone unturned to bring in
species culprits, 'none will be exempt'.

Sources:

A global assessment of all 826 known species of eucalypt trees – of which some 812 grow only in Australia – has found almost a quarter are threatened with extinction (International Union for Conservation of Nature). "As keystone species, [eucalypts] define the landscape of the entire Australian continent, and are culturally significant to its first nations people," the IUCN reported in 2019. Some 134 species of eucalypts had drops in numbers of at least 30% and the endangered Rose Mallee had declined by more than half.' Graham Readfearn, 'Almost a quarter of eucalypt trees found to be threatened with extinction', *The Guardian* online 11 December 2019, www.theguardian.com/environment/2019/dec/11/almost-a-quarter-of-eucalypt-trees-found-to-be-threatened-with-extinction#

Eucalyptus morrisbyi is listed as Critically Endangered under criteria A2a; C1+2a(i); D.' IUCN Redlist: Fensham, R., Laffineur, B. & Collingwood, T. 2019. E*ucalyptus morrisbyi*. *The IUCN Red List of Threatened Species* 2019: e.T30533A133031902. https://dx.doi.org/10.2305/IUCN.UK.2019-3.RLTS.T30533A133031902.en._Morrisby's gum is a small tree endemic to Tasmania's southeast. It is only known from two locations 21 km apart, the Government Hills near Risdon and the fragmented Cremorne subpopulation. The latter now consists of a main stand at Calverts Hill and several small remnant stands … The Risdon stand is now considered to be functionally extinct as it no longer produces seed. This leaves the species with fewer than 30 mature trees in the wild that produce seed.' https://nre.tas.gov.au/Documents/Eucalyptus-morrisbyi-listing-statement.pdf

'None will be exempt' is cited from 'Verdicts' — Dmitri Prigov (1940-2007). Translated, from the Russian, by Simon Schuchat with Ainsley Morse. I-print edition of *The New Yorker*, 3 February 3 2020, www.newyorker.com/magazine/2020/02/03/verdicts

Painted weather

Your meteorology app fails and you turn
to art's reliable confusions – clouds and seas,
moonscapes and desert Gethsemanes,
those pared-back, Umbrian beauties made
by Piero or Giotto, say. Paintings, dependable
as dogs in storms, frame dream atmospheres,
as if to say, look, see how unstable weather once blew
the roof off this or that Brueghelian peasant cottage
in Breda, not far from the tip, oh, about
five hundred years ago, townsfolk angling bodies
against bitter sleet that might at any time turn
into snow's soft, noiseless death,
the painter summoning multiple weathers
(not good science or glaciology per se),
something just as complicated and subtly felt.

Now the nightly weather girl/boy terrorises,
the dupe of 'natural cycles' refused with toothy cheer.
Your app restores; its wild-feed wisdoms beg you look
more closely at the space beyond art:
the poisoned river, the jaded lake of home.

You try working in a foreign city, but plug no charger
into its humid histories. Inside the disturbed museum,
weightless, paper-scrolled old weather is kept
in hushed, dark spaces. Meanwhile, the weather
of work and a short life are yours. You wear a new shirt
to the office, buttoned down under a dark December sky,
wet season lasting too long, draining a sulphurous fug
of frangipani and run-off through choked gutters.
One weekend you visit a lush river valley out of town.
The tropical overhang is postcard perfect, but the river
is orange, the stream a green anime. At dusk,

the water's chartreuse tints fade. You fill up
on the way home, your car garlanded by rainbows
of thin gasoline on concrete, industry's old art.
You'll revisit the river soon, sometime late
in the day and try your own hand at watercolour,
subtle impressions, as briefly felt as
a typhoon's deathly, dependable beauty.

The hay wain's cry

after John Constable's The Hay Wain (Landscape: Noon), *1821, National Gallery, London and Peter Kennard's* Haywain with Cruise Missiles, *1980 (Tate, London).*

They came for me then, biscuit-tin icon
of a green and pleasant land, shortbread cheap.
They papered me over with tarred millpond,
rust-limned clouds, machines blunted and unmanned.

Of a green and pleasant land, shortbread cheap,
I cannot speak (I risk poetic breach).
Rust-limned clouds, machines blunted and unmanned,
imperfect sky – beyond my varnished speech.

I cannot speak (I risk poetic breach)
of the art of the boy and girl who came,
imperfect sky – beyond my varnished speech,
the girl gluing soft hands to my gilt frame.

Of the art of the boy and girl who came,
as old guards swept sugar-high school groups out,
but not the girl, hands glued to my gilt frame,
facts cooed tremulous o'er the dirty Stour.

Old guards swept sugar-high school groups out
from talk of forty new oil and gas fields,
facts cooed tremulous o'er the dirty Stour.
'Elysium!' I cried, fear glossed. 'We shan't yield.'

O'er talk of forty new oil and gas fields,
we sang of old bones 'neath the tarred millpond.
'Elysium!' I cried, fear glossed. 'Do not yield.'
They came for me then, a biscuit-tin icon.

Note: On 5 July 2022, Hannah Hunt and Eben Lazarus glued themselves to the frame of *The Hay Wain* (original title *Landscape: Noon*) in the National Gallery, London. Hunt and Lazarus also pinned an imagined dystopian paper version of *The Hay Wain* over the painting. 'You can forget about our 'green and pleasant land' when further oil extraction will lead to widespread crop failures which means we will be fighting for food,' Hunt noted in 2022. (*The Guardian* 7 Dec, 2022). In 2024, British PM Keir Starmer and his Energy Secretary Ed Miliband ruled out giving oil and gas forms new licenses to drill off the Scottish coast with Miliband noting that 'clean energy we produce at home is cheaper than fossil fuels, and more secure because dictators can't control it.' (Abby Wallace and Andrew MacDonald, Politico online, Sept 10, 2024). Just Stop Oil activists who have now ceased interventions in museums and galleries.

You made the desert bloom

'My absence is entirely trees'
– Mahmoud Darwish

But I, Iris haynei, live on in a dark 'forest of solitudes',
like a weed down a well,
awaiting a piercing salvo of late sun
to restore surface albido and sentience.
Let me tell you, living is a two-sided scythe.
Once cellular feeling restores, I do not flower,
I cry out like some dim old poet of moss and brook
locked away for more years than she can count:
Where is the maquis scrubland of my forbears?
Why have the olive trees been clear-cut and burned,
the pretty Hebron springs defiled?

You say again that they have made the desert bloom,
but I see only the dark, thirsty forests of Odin
planted over ruins and uprooted olive farms.
A handshake EU deal, Madame President,
Lebensraum and terra nullius distort anew.
You admire the fake, beautiful forest, and miss me,
leafy survivor in my hectare of gloom.
But there are others, others like me.

I, Iris haynei see how new lookouts surveil
the stinking valley, the old Bedouin springs
now fed by runnels of sewage
where native anemones rise like hearts
loosened from old bodies.
I dare not stretch my outlawed roots
to sip from the sick spring;
I rely on dew and fortitude
while the last organic farmers

penny pinch to buy pesticides –
not antibiotics for coughing songs.

In the picturesque distance, bulldozers cover
the dump where Bedouin will be resettled.
Scrub species are banned, but not stern pine guards.
I chant my name as daylight fades. I once held hands
with my brothers and sisters and raced spring across
Samarian limestone until the pink sunset shone
like a proud mother upon our wild entanglements,
where small deer, rabbits and foxes thrived.

Why notch up crimes on dull soldierly bark?
Time is a flat chronicle unsuited to image-making.
I turn to sober facts: fired ecosystems,
brush elimination and herbicides,
pine imports as proxy land police.
I see I've lost your attention; the mythic forest
trumps, though desertification was myth all along.
Picnic signs complete the ruin.

Come, I await more like me, lonely Iris haynei!
You say they made the desert bloom, but
agriculture birthed in the Fertile Crescent.
Oh friends – Quercus coccifera and Pistacia terebrinthus
– how you once thrived here.

I urge you sowers of the one-eyed crop,
come sit with me in your man-made dark,
await a precious salvo of late sun
and there feel monoculture's lonely ache.

I say you will not flower there.

Notes:

Title: extracted from statement by President of the EU Ursula Van Der Leyen with Israeli Prime Minister Bennett in Jerusalem, published 14 June 2022: 'I do not have to tell you that the founders of your country have basically made crops spring up from the driest of deserts. You made the desert bloom.' Author: Directorate General for Neighbourhood and Enlargement Negotiations. https://neighbourhood-enlargement.ec.europa.eu, accessed 14 Dec 2024.

Iris haynei is the national Flower of Palestine.

'forest of solitudes': extracted from a short story by AB Yehoshua, 'Facing the forests', trans. Miriam Arad, *Jewish Quarterly*, vol. 18, no.1 (1970), 33, 36: 'This isn't a rustling forest but a very still one, like a graveyard. A forest of solitudes. The pine trees stand erect, slim, serious, like a company of new recruits awaiting their commander.'

Part 2: headfire

Pessimism

Some said that if I didn't get out
from under the rubble and walk,
I'd never build a house, take out a loan,
nurse the local stream to good health
or meet you for a trembling amber glass.
What could I achieve, lying under
a crush of mattressed stone?
What example would I set to friends
and family who'd looked to me
to survive irritant, hidden peas?

When they came with their megaphones
and starved sniffer dogs
to entreat Lazarus-like moves,
what I did not say was that after
experiencing so much slow weight
I felt happily pressed by rock and shadow;
I'd take the rap for non-princessy attitude,
an inability to imagine a correct future
and diagnose the exact location of the pea.
I could not say that under the rubble I'd found
the perfect antidote for gloom and sorrow,
perfect distance from brittle headlines
and mawkish elegy. Under my mattress
of stone and dust, I had become the pea itself,
something green and hard that would one day
roll around valleys of pistachio and olive trees
like an avuncular god. And so I had nothing
to worry about. This, I could say without words,
was the great opportunity of my death.

Boy as stone

As a child, I threw stones,
wounding water, air, glass,
crows and classmates,
the impulse to wound – biblical, basic.
One hoarded stone lacked wings and legs,
but I felt its atomic pulse as friendship,
its yearning to displace matter
a thing shared, though it was stronger
than my marrow throw, my puny dreams
of wax-winged flight. The day came
to test my polished friend.
Was it me or it that skimmed unfixed air
and water with serial bounce
before a subdued murky landing?
Did I care who or what I hurt
then as now? Did the soft lake feel?

Disown stoning, it begged, wordlessly,
as it flew, let time and space divest
cruelty, let all flight be love.

I never read the stone's worn meaning,
my ten-year-old will-to-power meant
I did not grasp igneous wisdom in plain sight.
I threw the stone blind; it threw me wise.
It flew from me and I fell back,
trophyless, a dint older, betrayed
by a brotherly discobolus. I stayed
angry with that stone for years,
its girly, supplicant burial.

There are plenty more to land,
my father told me. So long as you

don't smash windows or faces,
he added, putting the good book down.
Short advice, from a devout banker
of igneous time, a stern rock speaking.

My father didn't know my pockets
had already filled with pebbles
to throw, wound, haunt and drown,
that I'd throw stones all the days of my life.

Aubade: American supermarket

Time to get up, a mother calls to a son
with bum-fluffed lip and tender fulcrum,
assault rifle stashed under his bed
in pale-blue wool, conspirator branches
tapping and calling on glass.

He can't bear the brilliantined, bird-called
songs of morning, the democratic fall
of first sun, TV teeth flashing greetings
like puny explosions.

Before breakfast he tours online. Dark,
gnomic halls where hoax ogres troll
the 'crisis actors' of gun-toted 'scenes',
events fake as every moon landing.

Today the faded cornflowers on
his mother's dressing gown
and his father's military hair-part rile,
nothing calms the ticking
in his head, corrects the joy
of the aged dog on the mat,
his father's briefcase stare.

He'll show them he's as fake born
and as fake dead as all the rest.
The burnt blast of afternoon will
kill the 'gaudy, blabbing, remorseful day',
jam daybreak's glorious inbox still.

The wire door slams, crushes insect poetries;
he's on his way. Hollyhocks bend in his wake;

His mother cries: You take a sandwich baby?
At the town roundabout, the grand oak cracks,
calls him by name. Gelid skies divest warmth;
weather reports cry gloom inside
the hire car cab that cost everything.

Today he's everything before he's not:
trainers he can't afford, the smart car
nosing along nob hill. He is ogre and troll,
sprung from dank cave into livid daylight.
Airy goodness, its slow civic processionals
along supermarket aisles
six, seven, eight and nine, can't touch him.

When he emerges from his baby blanket,
the sum of all his parts and the butt,
he takes down sunlight, self and world
in the dazed dairy aisle.
His baby roars and day and night
pull apart forever, trolleys clack nowhere.
Outside, gimlet-eyed sun wonders
where the birds have gone;
rowed shops hold
each other up like sisters.
The register rolls on and on
unattended, the dead
receiptless. Mothers descend
to keen and fold, and fold again.
In dark halls, ogres cry fake.

Note: 'the gaudy, blabbing and remorseful day', from Shakespeare, Henry VI, Part 2, Act 4, Scene 1.

Petroleum

i.m. Hannah Clarke and children

Lights went on and off, but no one called;
no numbered car arrived to insist he go.
Dusk's violet mystery always reminded him,
or so he thought, of everywoman – her
palpable deceptions, cowardly assertions
and general inability to stay quiet.
Loneliness or low self-esteem had never
troubled him, he lied, that day in court.
He was a rugby star, bright and fast
as the first star of evening.
That was why he set out to candle
the birthrights of those he loved,
the wife who gave up a galactic mate.
He fanned a pure white heat,
raced it up and down the hill
the night long, looking for fuel,
refining a perfect, small-sided
contact game in a narrow channel.
Council lights flickered off
as dawn trapped and struck.
Meanwhile, domestic orders kindled
in a metal file three suburbs west
of the sun-filled new estate;
for history of anger and violence,
see sections 34.2 and 72.7D.

At 8.45am, the shouting man
broke the line and raced uphill.
Morning came, black and blue,
his school-bound family striking out
from the zone of home,

chrome duco holding them as
reflected cumulus, skied beauty.
It was then the sun blanked
his smiling son's belted view
of grinding trucks, toppled bins,
old Eric in faded dressing gown
hosing flame grevilleas, as the man
raced past, faster and faster,
match and jerrycan held aloft,
stride Olympian, a right rhythmic
prayer in his head sparking myth.

The boy's sisters, neat-plaited
and lunch-boxed, were first to see
their father crest the rise, their mother's
brow a u-turned concentration –
she'd forgotten to pack the apples.
The girls saw him run in front,
hesitate then strike a match
to raining birthday fuel,
tackling them all above
the shoulder line,
strategising forever love.

The hold

You schooled me to believe help comes, like love.
But sugared optimism fails when you
and the computer die in the same week.
I'm impatient with grief in order not to know it.
I fill my life with tasks.
Customer disservice candles spot-fires,
the threat of your return, waxen
in your good peony dress, shaking your head.
I'm call number ten, then seven, five and three.
One. I cross a virtual Styx, shout at
a quiet man named J, that I can't get in,
that I've lost everything. Does he get it?

J's voice is strangely gentle and kind,
as if he knows I'm no natural shouter.
As if he knows, too, that minutes before,
I gave up waiting and tipped out your old
overnight bag, rescued from the time-travel
dark of a dysfunctional cupboard, missed
by the cool, prying fingers of relatives.
There I found half-used, age-defying make-up;
powders and broken paste necklaces.
They coil at my feet, a familiar junk atoll
I'll need to bin. Are you still there?

J, the technician, tells me to browse the past,
delete all the old passwords blocking access,
You gotta clear keychains.
It's about preferences, love. Keep what you need.
I'll show you remotely. Here's a URL.
I clutch my arms, mimic a motherly clasp.
How to say: my mother was not a preference,
a clasper. Does J know this?

The remote voice consoles, a kind wizard.
I prepare to drown on my oceanic patch
of two-dollar-shop pearls. As we talk,
words re-string, beadlike, human tone
the colour of peonies.

You there? Sometimes we fix it, sometimes not.
He'll be sacked, this minion doubter.
He can't see me nodding, miming
ma-ma, ma-ma over your frayed bag.
I'm here. I'm here, I say, finally, but wait music
sets in, a tinny glossolalia. Then I have access,
keychains of scent, bead and word.

Is there anything else I can help you with today?

Decluttering

It took him twelve years to open the sealed vase
in the linen press, swathed and comforted, he liked to think,
by sheets and towels, flannels to wipe his kids' broken-pie faces,
covered in snot, tears and incoherent yearning. Making the beds up
was still his fortnightly shock; there was his wife, neat as a pin inside
the retro German vase, brown and orange glaze like overdone makeup,
the cannister urn-like enough – waisted, anthropomorphic.
Still, this was her. He didn't date again for six years. The first woman wrote
to reject him, saying she had proof single dads got more attention,
that he needed to open the lid, de-shrine the house. This was no simple
exercise in decluttering, though his wife had been a fan of Marie Kondo:
Commit yourself to tidying up; finish discarding first;
tidy by category, not by location; ask yourself if it sparks joy ...
He could not tidy by category; he stepped through milestone moments,
knowing she was there, smiling down in her granular wisdom, a giant jam jar
of grace, never spread nor placed. His sisters noted milestone memorial talk,
helped him draft words, ideas bubbling. He felt his way along,
a blindman inside a broom cupboard. Each time, he declined
the cookie-cutter monument, polished words a dull social security of grief.
The girl, as she grew, tortured him by default. She became her mother's
dead spit at twelve, chiding him, taking on the role of bedmaker,
high priestess of sheets and towels. She ignored the vase, while the boy
shrugged his shoulders re the rock, a mother barely known imprinted
on a brass plaque. Memorials lacked the angry potential of devices.
A rock? Something to bang your head against.
In the twelfth year of his solitude, the man opened
the door of the press to check the constant wife and mother
was still there – bedded in thread-counted cotton.
The opening of the jar coincided with the first day
of his daughter's last year at school. The day, blue-socked
and cloudless, let the future press in. He dropped her
at the school gate, smiling. But as he drove away,
he felt the sky open, raining rocks and boulders,

a cheap disaster movie. The roof of the car held.
The boulder storm passed; at home he contemplated
the plaqueless rock sitting pretty on the backyard ridge,
grass mown, wind-pegged sheets and towels thrashing,
dog racing past with stolen flannel, sparking joy.

Peacekeeping

Peace is rarely kept, as a man, woman or ledger is kept,
has nothing to do with beekeeping, though protective
suiting may enforce it. Peace is not kept like a sacrament
inside a tabernacle or casket. It is not 'kept nice'.
Knowing this, she secrets food, books, blankets and water bottles.
What she doesn't keep: a two-roomed house, three goats,
a quarter-share in a well, a husband taken in the night,
hands tied tight with electrical cords, captors
with one-week-old moustaches repeating:
You have not kept the faith, the faith.

Days later, by her rock-walled garden, they visit again.
You'll keep, they say in their language. She answers boldly:
Keep what? What? Her daughter plays in shadow
cast by spade and gun; books are no longer permitted.
That night, she sets out to a cousin's place in the mountains.
There, her uncle has an old TV, stuck on one channel.
The TV talks of 'implicit burden sharing
around the refugee problem'. She turns it off and rests.
She doesn't trust the box of static, or believe that the dead radio
will spring to life. She doesn't trust white-trucked UN convoys
snaking through the valley like signs of an enemy's prophet.

One morning, men appear at the pass below her uncle's house,
moving through his small flock with knives, Kalashnikovs,
and bundled cords. It is the keepers. She grabs her daughter,
takes off along the forest path behind the house. She brings a coil
of her uncle's best rope, something strong and slack.
After months running, in heat and cold, she comes close
to 'Europe', where, she's been told, ties and bridges can be made.
With others, she ties ropes together to cross a boiling river.
This entails many willing keepers, working both sides of the bank
to make a knotted trapeze. Oh lucky day! As she crosses

the flushing torrent, heart hammering, child a shrieking weight,
she thinks that this is what is meant by the English phrase
'running away to the circus'. People cheer, clap and shake,
crying out to the old ones, stranded a country apart.
On the other side, she lies down at a border as clean
and precise as a hair part. The air is fresh. She sleeps for hours
under a silver sheet, guarded by rows of spindly pines.

When she arrives at a camp, rich soil becomes stone
and pebble; a sprouting garden of bright plastic.
She keeps her peace about the stuffy NGO-issue tent,
but it is so hot, her dreams guy with new roped terrors.
Each day, she wakes, exhausted.
There's no news of her husband's lovely young eyes.
Goaty radio voices announce that, while peace has not come,
the dog remains hopeful on his chain. Politicians tour,
groomed faces sorrowing, as if to say, what is kept,
kept here, is burdensome. The tired clinic nurse,
mispronouncing their names, inoculates.
The psychologist suggests 'ritual patience',
though her daughter won't go to school alone,
and walls of plastic don't harden into a village.
She sleeps with a bar by the bed.

One day a message comes. The message
is for her alone, a chance of roped reunion.
She greets her daughter at the school with hugs,
knows she was right to keep her uncle's rope,
something strong and slack, a coiled future,
to cast over all the rivers on the planet.

Bread, lead and music

She buys bread at a 'safe place', down streets
of scaffold and scrim. No one stops her
for eight lead-cracked, potholed blocks.
Sweat rains down the small country of her back.
They say the music shop can be saved,
pale-shrouded, ritually virginal, as if angels or doctors,
not steel-collared mortars, reside therein.
No sign of the white-haired owner,
a three-war veteran. In a nearby skip,
three broken pianos converse, a polyphonics
of wire, black enamelled timber, ivory teeth.
The little bread shop next door lights up
at her approach, olfactories of golden dough
scent lead-shinned air. This is the safe place,
fat loaves the best kind of unexploded ordinance.
Today, the street's devoid of commercial jingles,
but ecstatic piano – Chopin or Liszt
(she can't pick which) – blast flaked paint
from under the builders' scrim, the street
a briefly shaken, snowdomed loveliness,
and free concert for all. The queue's a glad mess –
heads rise to the notes, one chaotic, unkneaded
organism. They've not heard music for months,
or is it years? Tempo, like history, so wounded
by vestibular impairment that nothing conducts.
But wait! A new century of bullet holes fills
with music, plaster and dough; that is to say, 'future'.

In the caul of this new future, no-one's picky
about gluten-free variations or accurate
period reconstruction. Material shapes
restore in altered casts. Rhythm, harmony
and counterpoint prove memory's yeast.

The great street fugue swells until ghosts
release from split beams and cornices to join
the queue, softly tapping her shoulder
to say: 'I knew your mother, didn't I?'
'My grandmother', she corrects, smiling.
She waits for the hair-netted woman to wrap
her sour loaf in soft shrouds and thinks
she's in hospital again. Outside, workmen
whistle and shadow-play behind the scrim,
repair the facade for her delectation.
Recorded, painterly notes rain down
for her open-mouthed wonderment.
She walks away, bread warm against
her chest, head bent to miracles
of fair supply, the ancient balm
of bread and music.

Museum of the future

Hong Kong, November 2023

I'm too tall for the sixties arcade
where aircon stutters like foreigners
mouthing business-card Cantonese.
Shop cells crammed with jade, umbrellas,
clocks and tailors' suiting tell of slow time
between revolution and occupation.
A thin-haired man in crisp white shirt
sells me an old Seiko alarm clock,
a cure for late-night doomscrolling.
It's an Olympic model, he says, smiling.
Early digital, used for track and field.
He laughs as if time has run out, onsold
to an eternal digital present, grander forces.
What about a watch? he asks, half-hopeful
in front of polished wall-to-wall old stock,
wristwatches too heavy for ghosts.
Everyone has phones now, I say, apologetic.
He nods ruefully. Hard to sell, yes, hard to sell!
The mechanisms are beautiful, he calls after me.

*

On Shantung Street, red bunting and neon
blood the eye; the 74th anniversary of
the People's Republic flutters and blinks.
Inside the museum, a former prison,
children flee though slim exhibits,
wall text gaps, gaps in time.
Selected objects and props
may be touched, but tactile history
is fifteen minutes long.

See the salted fish counter c. 1920;
try out standard-issue tiny furniture c. 1952.
It's like grandma's, but smaller, a child cries,
puzzled by scatter-gun time, doll-like chairs,
the scentless simulacra of a fishing haul.
No talk of umbrellas opening like flowers
on crowded Civic Square, the sleepy terror
of minors detained at educational bootcamp,
harbour glitz, a techno-feudalist pageant.

*

I retreat to Kowloon cool, hotel room
redolent of a cigarette century,
street noise double-glazed two-star.
My new–old clock, bright yellow with hope
on the veneered side table, stays quiet,
but there's a ticking inside my head.
At dinner, an expat friend says,
If you don't poke the bear,
you can have a good life here.
At the universities, groomed mainlanders
enrol as classroom plants. They always
forget their umbrellas, the opening of things.
Who cares about a little rain, they say,
chat vociferous, cavalier, forging
'deep connection'. Vague about Canto
culture, they are schooled in the future's
beautiful dogmatic mechanism.
Outside, typhoon warnings upgrade,
brollies open and close,
caught in windblown cul-de-sacs.

Laundromat

In the wash church, smalls decode,
sheeted love and loss cram in.
What is, or was, at stake, is soaped
under violent chemical scrutiny.
On unbearable centrifugal afternoons,
the tight, hot room gives too much away.
A machine stops and renders the music of
the neat young man with ear bud and rash,
black-clad self washed over and over;
a saint-faced Ethiopian woman wrangles
children hunting hot pink socks
in humid echochambers.
Outside, a junkie tethers
his needle-eyed mutt to the broken kerb,
slides in to wash his shadow clean.
The lined man on TPV searches
his four-season overcoat
for coins and stories of all
the revolutions he has seen,
the old spin and fall, careful
to leave nothing behind in case
he's asked to leave again.

Come late evening, the manager folds
hoodies, lone socks and underpants,
tender philanthropies fill an hour,
greyed-out, elasticised items
sagging like politicians' words.
Meanwhile, no-one knows the owner
of the forlorn, deer-patterned pyjama top,
who'll go cold this night and every other night
they don't return, riding a sleigh

across the moon in the buff, checking
every place they went but here.

At 10pm, gibbous moon pearling
into view, the manager locks
the shop's bright loneliness
against the pilled, hooded night.

Low cloud in the gentleman's park

after Jacob Van Ruisdael's View of the Ruins of Huister Kleef and Haarlem, *c. 1660s, Musée Jacquemart André, Paris*

She did not inherit pictures nor cash.
But land she inherited a plenty,
adjacent to his family's stony holding.
Once the loveless knot was tied
and beringed, her land became his.
Thirty years separated them,
a low stone fence, easily leapt.

She'd known his cold pile of rock,
set low in the valley, since childhood,
Faux-Palladian style all wrong,
ceilings too high for heating.
Wind whistled though as she sat.
Songs of older female sorrows
shrilled tunelessly under stone vaults.
By the gallery's mean, pretty fire
she ruminated on the production of heirs.
that kind of musing a given, alongside
samplers and watercolours.

She sat for hours among portraits
of her husband's long-faced kin,
stays drawn tight, life upholstered
to the velvet balloon back.
The pictures that struck her most
(a different strike to his backhander)
were gentlemen's parks, beautifully crafted,
for a price, even for the ungentlemanly.
Tree-filled vistas were divested of slaves,

but not slavery's cruel profits, porticoes
haloed by burls of cottony cloud.

Her lonely eighteen years were thus
constrained. Weather belonged to men
(who made and influenced it),
as ewes belonged to rams, though now
her husband owned her sheep as well.
Early on, she found she was with child.
Her flat chest ached; no food stayed down.
A weathered portrait artist arrives
to fix her youth in oil and linseed
inside a carapace of silk and ermine.
At sittings, she wore her mother's jewels,
his mother's faded family sash.
Wan as celadon, the painter shades
madder below dead plum eyes.
Her husband will not hang it, his theft
and bruise displayed for all to see.

The birth was difficult. The life intolerable.
One day, she left the child with a wet nurse.
In the gallery, she lifted down a
flatland landscape by van Ruisdael.
Aah! She'd cherished the open space
achieved by so intimate a scale; now it
depressed her. She'd no chance to step
through and past marbled storm clouds.
Space and time constrained – her life,
a cut-glass trophy of wintry nothing.

She looked one last time at the painting,
the massive low-weighted cloud soon to drop
like the bundled rear of a giant tear-soaked
infant on five acres of perfectly good cabbages

and brought scissors from her pocket.
She had not expected a second child so soon.

This was her life, that of a perfectly good cabbage,
heritable jewellery worn over the florets.
Cutting up the painting was a small revenge,
the cabbage speaking up for herself.
She fed it to the mean, pretty fire,
ash and provenance swirling up the flue.
Melted medium gave up a smell of libraries.
The gilt frame went next. Then nothing.
A naked square of light on grand,
soot-dark stone impugned.

At the stables, her husband's favourite stallion,
Black Orion, pawed fearfully at his stall, alert
to smoke and history. The mistress got dressed
and took her crop. She'd ride the wild horse hard
while her husband gambled ram and ewe away
in London, resting nights on other downy pillows.
She'd ride the stars until she fell, and the moon
salved the bruises she'd inherited,
the cut-up landscape of a child.

The colour of fog

after Claude Monet, Thames embankment views (series), 1901

You woke, scratched your ample arse and abluted,
looked askance at the tray of grey, buttered haddock
and mud-pond coffee – no good cure for Alice,
her colourless fog rivalling the vaporous street,
filling formal room after formal room.
You too are half-smothered by loss,
a stepdaughter singing soil under Giverny lime.
Quick! Convert airless memory into earth tone:
Van Dyke brown, burnt umber, raw … raw.
But you hated those hues. The English city miasma
made Alice cough up browns. Modern grief,
a good thing, progress. Pure raw umber.
You took cigars in the hidebound lobby
where smoke coiled and purred around
the felt shoulders of industry scions,
your son Michel profiting brown English verbs:
win, pay, produce, modernise, control, collect.
Oh yes, Messieurs, my lovely mother collects art.

That's what you did back then. Cashed up,
you booked two rooms at the Savoy, one to sleep in,
one to paint in, relying on a smog-sweetened palette
for your 'effets': Waterloo Bridge, Parliament,
factory chimneys and a catheterised Thames
steeped in purple, mauve and yellow –
the sfumato poisons of new capital.
Most days fog baffles the catarrh
of workers hugging the bridges,
dye-vat lungs flecked blue and vermillion,
as evening and the robust obfuscations
of the phlegmatic class close in.

When the jaundiced air grows quiet
you boil up rabbit-skin glue on the burner,
tighten eighty canvases into resounding drums
of the world, oblivious to chambermaid eyerolls
as foul fugs leach down velvet corridors.
Grief, or intolerance of grief, provokes
the serial images friend Pissarro will chastise.
London riverside on repeat? Mad!
When you crate them up to send home, half-finished,
Alice rises in her bed, ghost hands searching your face,
but suddenly happy, happy as an opium poppy.

En route to Dover, train smoke's an unusable no colour.
Distracted, you smooth Alice's black brows away.
At home, you finish each work from memory,
just before your first lillied consolations erupt.
The debt to your English 'veils' is bridal:
whites, pinks and mauves, landscape fogged.
Alice, listless in the hammock, nods, catching sun
in her hair, seven children gathering to pull at her
as if she were a loom they would prise apart,
her darling luddites, seeking flesh, cloth, bone
and equitable love. Her impossible canvas.

And you, cataract-frantic on Nympheas n°s 91 and 92,
failing to see or hear her, grafting a moody dash
of English smog to your living, ponded world,
bodily machine still bright as a gas lamp,
underpainting fading in the artless dusk
like giftshop tea towels out of time.

Rollerblading

i.m. David Berman

I once had a favourite poem of milk and honey,
full of love and amity, the kind of poem you read
when things grow tough, and even the dog
does not 'reach out'. In that moment, I reached
for the new sincerity. Or even the old.
I basted in that poem's milk and honey, its sugared
Californian optimism – amber beer in sunlight,
baseball mitts, the prettiest beach sunset imaginable,
a live painting awaiting the rollerblading 'one',
only faintly suspicious you'd shoved irony,
a late seaside carnival, deftly out of frame.

I did not heed the lank gull's caution.
When you suicided, I felt cheated.
Hadn't you written that poem to save yourself,
mood swings painted out by candy skies,
your dear friend Chuck's earnest bifocals sending
starry glints of loving kindness out into the universe?

I'd wanted that world. Then you taught
me that the optimistic poem was pure
entrapment, a gaudy bauble. Don't gild
the lily or it will gild you, your coffin sprung
open full of cheesy words and poor rhyme schemes.

I did not make the funeral nor read reprints
of wintry elegies made by friends and colleagues.
I'm sure the weather was bad that day,
relatives bored, preacher a hand-clappy dud.
If I'd been there, I'd have said a line
is the only optimism. But you knew that.

You saw both sides, held the line awhile.
You knew that, if you were lucky, you'd be dealt
a few Disney days: baseball, cold beer, love
and radiance bursting forth over a sandy desk,
a few good poems rollerblading into the sunset.

Acknowledgements

This work was made variously on beautiful Wurundjeri and Gadabanud country. My grateful thanks go to the following wonderful journal editors and publishers: Jessica Wilkinson, Peter Rose, John Hawke and Katherine McLean. 'The sentence' was published in Rabbit 40 (Extinction issue, guest editors Elena Gomez and aj carruthers); 'Painted weather' in Australian Book Review, no. 454; 'Setting the table' in Australian Poetry Anthology (guest editors Andy Jackson, Marcella Polain), volume 11, 2024; 'Controlled burn' and 'The woman who ran the farm' in the 2024 Newcastle Poetry Prize Anthology. 'The hold' and 'Decluttering' were shortlisted in the 2023 ACU Poetry Prize and appeared in that year's anthology. 'Bread, lead and music' and 'Peacekeeping' were shortlisted in the 2022 ACU Poetry Prize and were similarly anthologised in that year.

Especial thanks to my best and most generous reader, Anthony Lynch. Other poets and writers have provided encouragement with drafts and individual poems, spurring me on when doubts arose. My profound thanks to Brendan Ryan, Marion May Campbell, Deborah Wardle, Shari Kocher, Suzy Freeman-Greene and others. Special thanks to Tracy Ryan and Andy Jackson for reading this manuscript and providing such thoughtful recommendations. Last but not least, I thank Dr David Musgrave, fine poet and publisher at Puncher & Wattmann, for committing to another book of mine.

www.ingramcontent.com/pod-product-compliance
Ingram Content Group Australia Pty Ltd
76 Discovery Rd, Dandenong South VIC 3175, AU
AUHW021522130126
422047AU00001B/3

9 781923 099708